Popcorn Bucket

Cupcakes and Muffins

Fruit Basket

Ice Cream Cones

Pizza Slices

Sandwich

Candy and Sweets

Vegetable Garden

Pancakes and Waffles

Cookies

Milk Shake

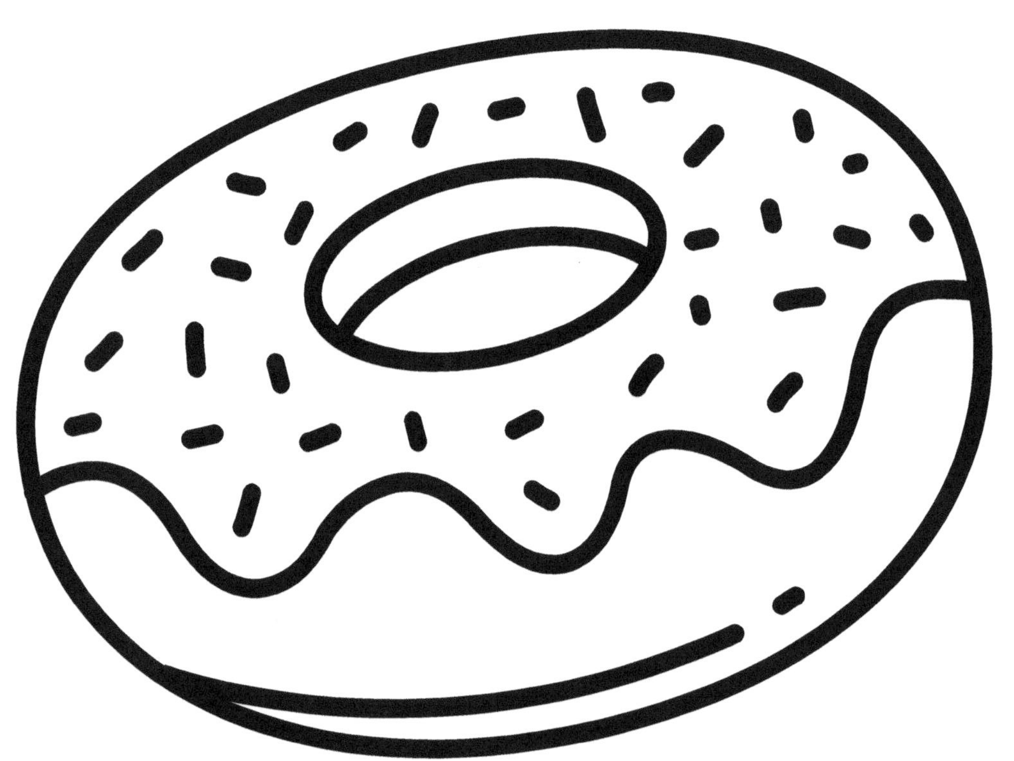

Doughnut

French Fries

Yogurt

Nuts

Peanut

Butter

Potato Chips

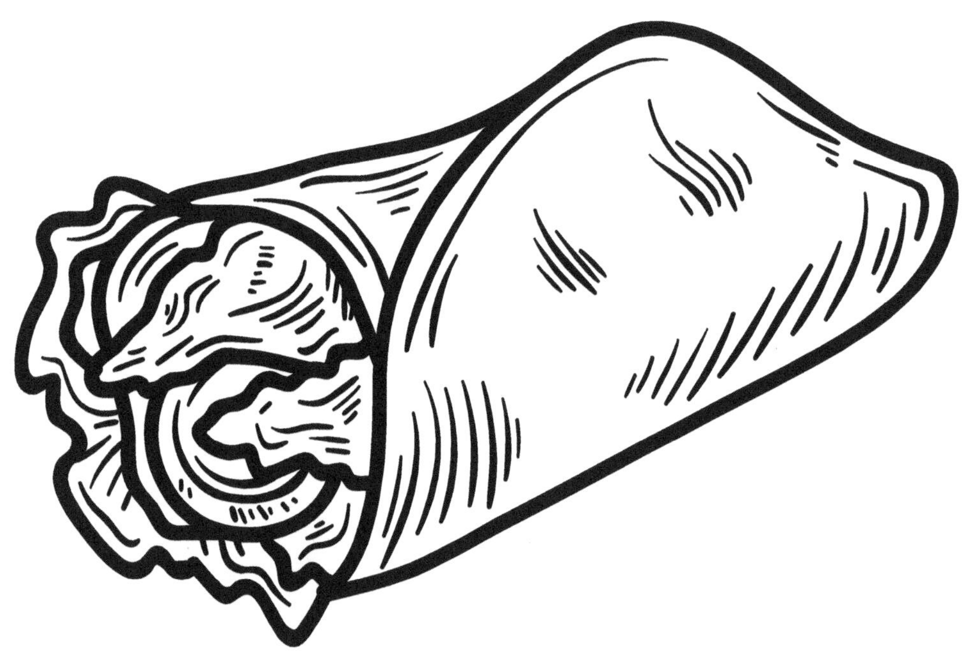

Wrap

Pastry

Fruit Salad

Butter

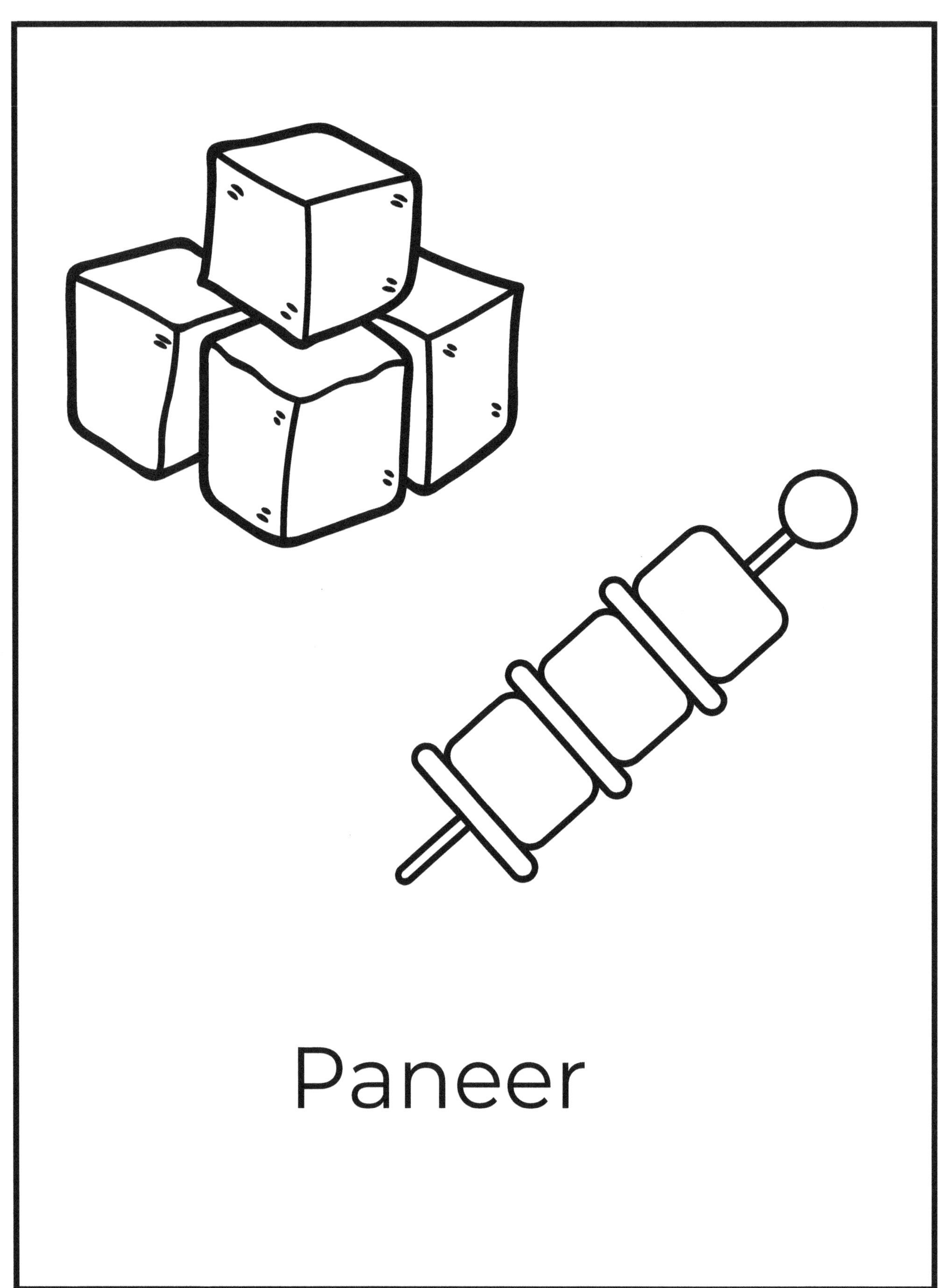

Paneer

Burger

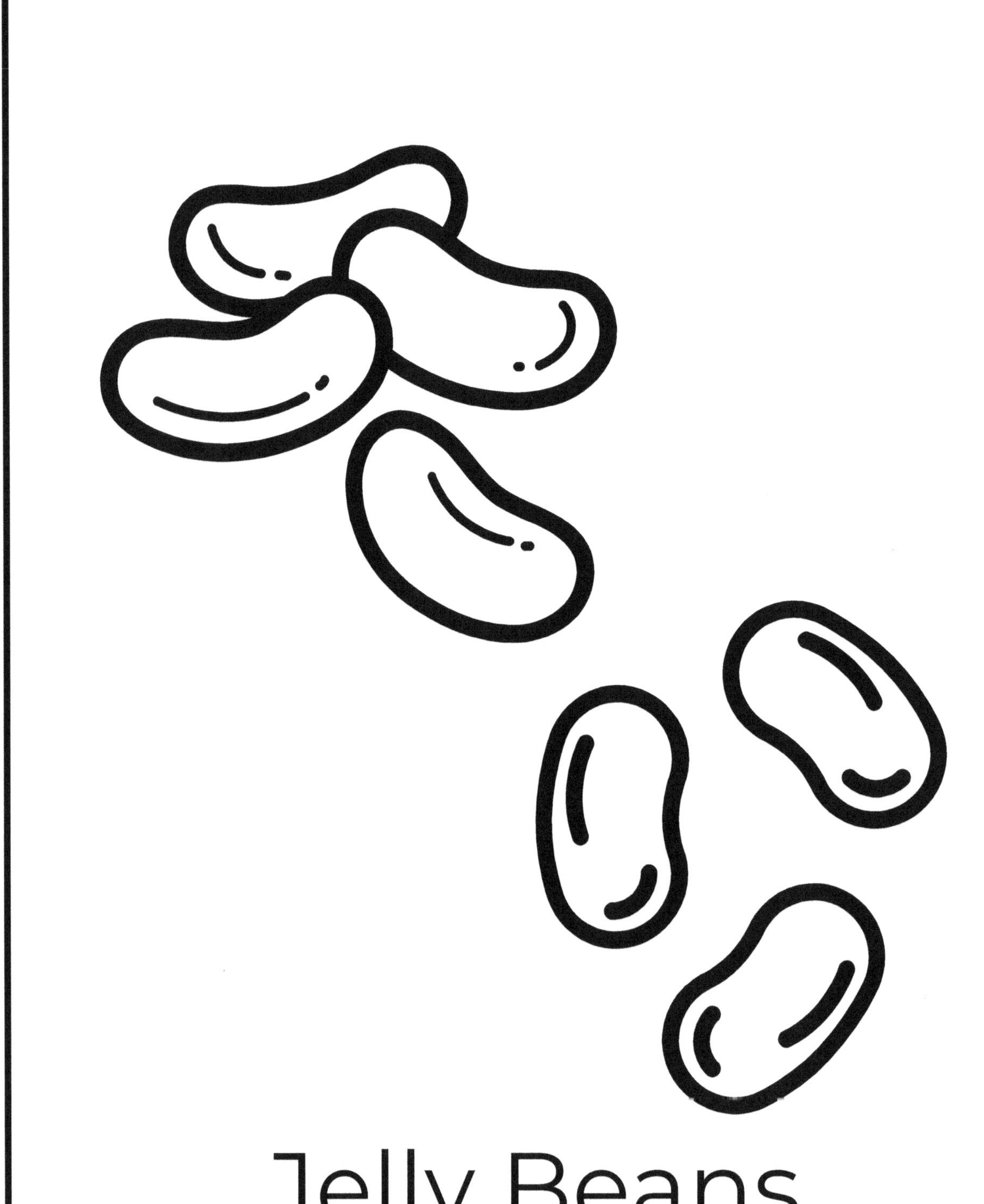

Jelly Beans

Noodles

Rice Bowl

Taco

Bagel

Sushi

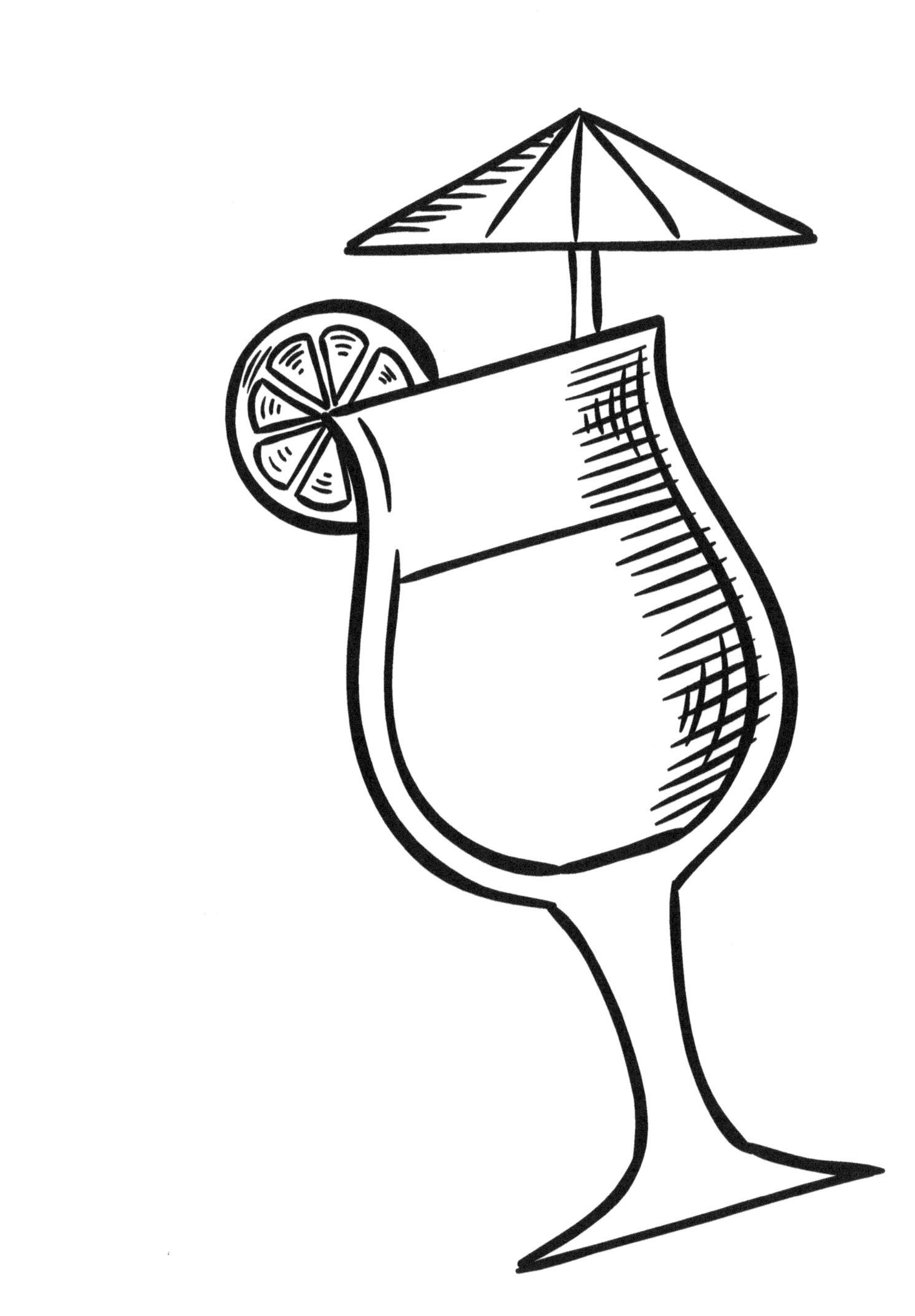

Summer Drink